Last Breath:A Tale of Survival in the

Last Breath: A Survival in the Depths

The True Story of Chris Lemons' Fight for Life in the North Sea and the Human Spirit's Unyielding Will to Overcome Extreme Danger

Angel O. Brien

Copyright Information

Copyright © by Angel O. Brien2025. All rights reserved.

Before this document is duplicated or reproduced in any manner, the publisher's consent must be gained. Therefore, the contents within can neither be stored electronically, transferred nor kept in a database. Neither in part or full can the document be copied, scanned, faxed or retained without approval from the publisher or creator.

Table of Contents

Copyright Information

Table of Contents

Introduction

Chapter One
Synopsis of the Documentary (2019)

Chapter Two
Synopsis of the Feature Film (2025)

Chapter Three
Themes and Messages in Last Breath

Chapter Four
Analysis of the Documentary Last Breath (2019)

Chapter Five
Analysis of the Feature Film Last Breath (2025)

Chapter Six
Comparative Review: Documentary vs. Feature Film; Last Breath (2019 vs. 2025)

Chapter Seven
Character Exploration; Last Breath (2019 Documentary vs. 2025 Feature Film)

Chapter Eight
Cinematography and Visual Style; Last Breath (2019 Documentary vs. 2025 Feature Film)

Chapter Nine
Emotional and Psychological Impact; Last Breath (2019 Documentary vs. 2025 Feature Film)

Chapter Ten
Lessons and Takeaways from Last Breath (2019 Documentary & 2025 Feature Film)

Chapter Eleven
Cultural and Societal Impact of Last Breath (2019 Documentary & 2025 Feature Film)

Chapter Twelve
Critical Reception and Reviews of Last Breath (2019 Documentary & 2025 Feature Film)

Conclusion
Final Thoughts on Last Breath as a Compelling Story of Survival

Last Breath:A Tale of Survival in the Depths

Introduction

The gripping story of Last Breath has captured the attention of audiences worldwide, first as a 2019 documentary and soon as a dramatized feature film set for release in 2025. Both versions recount the harrowing real-life ordeal of saturation diver Chris Lemons, whose life hung in the balance after a catastrophic underwater accident. While the documentary offers a raw and authentic glimpse into the perilous world of deep-sea diving, the feature film seeks to bring this extraordinary tale to a wider audience through dramatic retelling and star-studded performances. This introduction sets the stage for an exploration of Last Breath, examining its relevance, emotional depth, and the universal themes it conveys.

Overview of Last Breath (2019 Documentary and 2025 Feature Film)
The Last Breath documentary, directed by Richard da Costa and Alex Parkinson, recounts

the 2012 incident in which Chris Lemons became stranded 100 meters underwater in the North Sea. After his umbilical cable was severed, cutting off his oxygen supply and communication with the surface, Lemons faced an unimaginable fight for survival with just a few minutes of air remaining. The documentary employs real footage, interviews, and recreations to immerse viewers in the tension and stakes of this life-or-death scenario, highlighting the risks saturation divers face and the resilience required to endure such situations.

Building on the success of the documentary, the 2025 feature film, directed by Alex Parkinson, expands the narrative into a survival thriller. Starring Woody Harrelson, Simu Liu, Finn Cole, Cliff Curtis, and Djimon Hounsou, the film dramatizes the events with high-intensity visuals and emotional performances. While it retains the core essence of Lemons' story, it also explores the broader dynamics of teamwork, courage, and the human spirit in the face of overwhelming odds. The adaptation underscores the universal appeal of the story, transforming a niche diving incident into a compelling tale of endurance for global audiences.

Importance of the Story and Its Real-Life Basis

The true story of Chris Lemons is both extraordinary and relatable, making it a tale that resonates with people from all walks of life. The 2012 incident sheds light on the high-risk profession of saturation diving, an occupation that remains largely unknown to the general public. Lemons' ordeal not only illustrates the dangers inherent in this line of work but also highlights the importance of trust, expertise, and quick decision-making in life-threatening situations.

This story also serves as a testament to human resilience and survival instincts. Despite being trapped in the depths of the ocean with no immediate hope of rescue, Lemons managed to defy the odds and survive, a feat that astonished his colleagues and the wider world. The narrative is a reminder of the fragility of life and the incredible capacity of humans to endure and persevere.

Preview of the Themes Explored in the Movie
Last Breath delves deeply into themes of survival, teamwork, and the power of hope. It examines the psychological toll of isolation and fear while emphasizing the importance of unity and trust in high-pressure situations. Additionally, the story explores the fragility of human life in the face of nature's immense power, prompting viewers to reflect on their own lives and relationships. Ultimately, Last Breath is a celebration of the indomitable human spirit, offering inspiration through one man's incredible journey against all odds.

Chapter One

Synopsis of the Documentary (2019)

Last Breath (2019) is a deeply immersive documentary that recounts the real-life ordeal of saturation diver Chris Lemons, whose life was thrust into peril during a routine underwater operation in the North Sea. Directed by Richard da Costa and Alex Parkinson, the film is a powerful exploration of survival against overwhelming odds. Combining real footage, interviews, and reenactments, the documentary takes the audience into the high-pressure, high-risk world of saturation diving, where precision and teamwork are paramount.

Through its gripping narrative, Last Breath explores the physical, emotional, and psychological toll of being trapped in the ocean's depths. The film offers a profound look at the fragility of human life in an unforgiving environment and celebrates the resilience of the human spirit in the face of unimaginable challenges.

Plot Summary and Key Events
The documentary begins by introducing the audience to the unique and hazardous profession of saturation diving, where divers live in pressurized environments for weeks to perform deep-sea maintenance and construction tasks. Saturation divers rely on an umbilical cable connected to their diving bell to provide them with oxygen, communication, and heating. This lifeline is critical for their survival in the crushing depths of the ocean.

In September 2012, Chris Lemons, along with his colleagues Duncan Allcock and David Yuasa, embarked on a routine underwater maintenance task on an oil rig in the North Sea. What began as a standard mission quickly spiraled into disaster when the vessel supporting their operation lost dynamic positioning due to a catastrophic computer failure. This malfunction caused the ship to drift, severing Chris's umbilical cable and leaving him stranded 100 meters (328 feet) underwater in near-total darkness.

The plot focuses on the unfolding crisis as Chris is left with only a small emergency oxygen tank, which could sustain him for approximately five to seven minutes. Without communication or a reliable way to locate him, his crewmates scramble to rescue him in a race against time. Meanwhile, Chris, tethered to a fixed point, must confront the reality of his dire situation, all while battling the extreme cold, darkness, and crushing isolation of the deep sea.

The heart-stopping tension builds as Duncan and David, supported by the surface team, work desperately to maneuver the diving bell back to Chris's location. The stakes are incredibly high: every passing minute decreases his chances of survival. The documentary captures this life-or-death drama with a mix of real footage and expertly crafted reenactments, immersing the audience in the unfolding crisis.

Against all odds, after more than 30 minutes without a functioning oxygen supply, Chris is miraculously found alive. His survival defies both logic and medical understanding, leaving even the most experienced divers and experts stunned. The film concludes by reflecting on this extraordinary event and the bond between Chris and his colleagues, whose determination and teamwork saved his life.

Introduction to Chris Lemons and the North Sea Incident

Chris Lemons, a highly skilled saturation diver, is at the heart of the Last Breath story. Known for his calm demeanor and technical expertise, Chris was an integral part of a close-knit diving team tasked with performing underwater maintenance on oil rigs. The documentary paints a vivid portrait of Chris as both a professional and a person, exploring his background, relationships, and the qualities that made him a valued member of his team.

The North Sea, where the incident occurred, is one of the most challenging environments for saturation divers. Known for its unpredictable weather and strong currents, the region demands exceptional skill, preparation, and teamwork. On that fateful day in September 2012, Chris and his team faced one of the profession's worst nightmares; a loss of dynamic positioning on the support vessel. This technical failure caused the ship to drift uncontrollably, snapping Chris's lifeline and leaving him stranded in the ocean's depths.

The film delves into the specifics of the incident, offering a detailed account of the technical and human errors that compounded the crisis. It also highlights the profound trust and camaraderie among Chris and his colleagues, who risked their own lives to bring him back to safety. Through interviews and firsthand accounts, the audience gains a deeper understanding of the high-stakes world of saturation diving and the extraordinary circumstances surrounding Chris's survival.

Emotional and Survival Aspects of the Story

At its core, Last Breath is a story of human resilience and the will to survive. The emotional weight of the film lies in its portrayal of Chris Lemons' ordeal, as well as the desperate efforts of his team to rescue him. Stranded alone in the pitch-black abyss of the ocean, Chris faced an overwhelming sense of isolation and fear. The documentary captures these emotions with striking realism, drawing viewers into his experience.

Chris's survival hinged on a combination of factors, including his ability to remain calm under pressure and the extraordinary determination of his team. Despite knowing that his emergency oxygen supply would run out in minutes, Chris chose to focus on conserving energy and maintaining hope. This mental fortitude played a crucial role in his ability to withstand the dire conditions.

The film also explores the emotional toll on Chris's colleagues, who were forced to grapple with the possibility of losing a teammate. Their efforts to rescue Chris reflect not only their professional commitment but also the deep personal bond they shared. The tension and urgency of their actions are palpable, making the eventual success of their mission all the more impactful.

Beyond the immediate crisis, Last Breath examines the psychological aftermath of the incident for Chris and his team. The film offers an intimate look at how they processed the experience, from the trauma of the near-tragedy to the gratitude and relief of Chris's miraculous survival.

The documentary's emotional resonance extends beyond the individuals involved, inviting viewers to reflect on broader themes of life, mortality, and human connection. It is a powerful reminder of the fragility of existence and the strength of the human spirit, even in the most extreme circumstances.

The 2019 documentary Last Breath is a masterful blend of tension, emotion, and inspiration. Through its meticulous recounting of Chris Lemons' harrowing experience, the film sheds light on the unique challenges of saturation diving and the extraordinary resilience required to survive in such a hostile environment. By focusing on the emotional and survival aspects of the story, Last Breath transcends its niche subject matter to deliver a universally compelling narrative about hope, courage, and the power of human connection.

Chapter Two

Synopsis of the Feature Film (2025)

The 2025 feature film adaptation of Last Breath, directed by Alex Parkinson, takes the compelling true story of saturation diver Chris Lemons and elevates it into a dramatized survival thriller for a broader audience. Building on the foundation laid by the 2019 documentary, the film brings the harrowing events of Lemons' near-death experience to life with a star-studded cast, cutting-edge visuals, and a deeply emotional narrative. Starring Woody Harrelson, Simu Liu, Finn Cole, Cliff Curtis, and Djimon Hounsou, the movie expands on the original story by exploring the human connections, emotional stakes, and psychological depth of the crisis.

Set against the hostile and unforgiving backdrop of the North Sea, the film captures the tension and danger of saturation diving, immersing viewers in a life-or-death situation that tests the limits of human endurance. While staying true to the core events of Lemons' ordeal, the feature film introduces dramatized elements to enhance the storytelling and provide a richer, more cinematic experience.

Comparison with the Documentary

The documentary Last Breath (2019) presented an authentic and raw recounting of the 2012 incident, relying on real footage, interviews, and reenactments to convey the tension and stakes. Its primary focus was on the facts of the event and the emotional impact on those involved. By contrast, the 2025 feature film takes a more expansive and creative approach, dramatizing key moments to heighten the intensity and broaden the appeal.

One significant difference lies in the portrayal of Chris Lemons. While the documentary used interviews and voiceovers to present Chris as a real-life professional and survivor, the film delves deeper into his personal life, including his relationships and motivations. This approach makes him a more relatable and emotionally compelling character for the audience.

The feature film also amplifies the tension through dramatic pacing and visual effects, recreating the underwater environment with cutting-edge technology. Unlike the documentary, which focused on the real-world mechanics of saturation diving, the movie leans into cinematic storytelling techniques to create a more suspenseful and immersive experience.

The supporting characters in the film also receive expanded roles. The documentary highlighted the teamwork and camaraderie among Chris's colleagues, but the feature film delves into their individual backstories, emotions, and personal struggles during the crisis. This added depth enhances the narrative and makes the stakes feel even more significant.

Expanded Narrative and Dramatized Elements

To transform the story into a cinematic thriller, the filmmakers introduced several expanded narrative elements. The feature film explores Chris Lemons' life before the accident, including his relationships with his family and fiancée. These moments provide a poignant contrast to the life-threatening ordeal he faces underwater and give the audience a stronger emotional connection to his character.

The dramatization also includes fictionalized dialogue and moments that may not have occurred in the actual event. For instance, scenes of Chris reflecting on his life, imagining conversations with loved ones, or battling hallucinations due to oxygen deprivation add psychological depth to his character. These creative liberties allow the audience to experience his fear, hope, and determination on a more visceral level.

The film also heightens the role of the crew members on the surface and their frantic efforts to rescue Chris. While the documentary highlighted their teamwork and technical expertise, the movie dramatizes their personal conflicts, moments of doubt, and emotional toll. For example, Woody Harrelson's portrayal of the dive supervisor emphasizes the weight of responsibility he feels, while Simu Liu's character as a diver showcases the physical and emotional strain of navigating the dangerous rescue operation.

Visually, the movie takes full advantage of its medium to recreate the perilous underwater environment. The scenes of Chris stranded in the pitch-black depths of the North Sea, illuminated only by the flickering light of his headlamp, are both haunting and beautiful. The use of sound design, including muffled breathing, creaking equipment, and the eerie silence of the ocean, adds to the immersive experience.

Key Highlights and Differences
The feature film's key highlights lie in its ability to take a factual story and transform it into a cinematic spectacle. By expanding on the narrative and introducing dramatized elements, the movie provides a deeper emotional and psychological exploration of the events.

1. Character Development:
Chris Lemons' character is given a rich backstory, allowing the audience to see him as a person beyond his profession. The film portrays his love for his fiancée, his aspirations, and his inner thoughts during the crisis.

The supporting cast is also fleshed out, with each crew member facing personal dilemmas and emotional challenges as they work to save Chris.

2. Visual and Technical Excellence:

The film's underwater scenes are a standout feature, capturing the claustrophobic and dangerous environment with stunning detail.

Special effects are used to simulate the disorienting effects of oxygen deprivation and the crushing pressure of the deep sea, adding to the tension.

3. Dramatic Pacing:
The film intensifies the pacing of the rescue operation, intercutting between Chris's struggle to survive and the surface team's frantic efforts to locate him.

Moments of reflection and stillness are juxtaposed with high-stakes action, creating a rollercoaster of emotions.

4. Themes and Emotional Impact:
While the documentary focused primarily on survival and teamwork, the film delves deeper into themes of love, sacrifice, and the fragility of life.

The added emotional layers make the movie more accessible to a general audience, even those unfamiliar with saturation diving.

5. Dramatized Elements:
Scenes of Chris imagining conversations with loved ones or experiencing flashbacks provide insight into his mental state, even if they may not be entirely factual.

The film includes moments of tension and conflict among the crew that are amplified for dramatic effect.

The 2025 feature film adaptation of Last Breath succeeds in taking a powerful true story and crafting it into a gripping cinematic experience. By expanding the narrative, deepening character development, and utilizing cutting-edge visuals, the film enhances the emotional and psychological impact of Chris Lemons' harrowing ordeal.

While the documentary offered a raw and authentic portrayal of the events, the movie broadens the story's appeal by adding dramatized elements and exploring universal themes of survival, love, and resilience. The key differences between the two formats highlight the strengths of each medium: the documentary's realism versus the film's emotional depth and visual spectacle. Together, they provide complementary perspectives on a story that continues to inspire audiences worldwide.

Chapter Three

Themes and Messages in Last Breath

The story of Last Breath, whether in its 2019 documentary form or the 2025 feature film adaptation, is deeply resonant because of the powerful themes and messages it conveys. At its core, the story is about survival against all odds, human resilience, and the unshakable bonds of teamwork and trust in high-risk professions. These themes elevate the narrative beyond a mere survival tale, offering universal lessons about the human spirit and our capacity to overcome extraordinary challenges.

Survival Against All Odds

Survival is the heart of the Last Breath story, capturing the raw struggle of a man faced with seemingly insurmountable odds. Chris Lemons' ordeal in the North Sea; a place as dangerous as it is isolating, serves as a stark reminder of the fragile boundary between life and death. When Lemons became stranded underwater with only five minutes of breathable air and no immediate rescue in sight, his survival seemed almost impossible. Yet, his ability to endure more than 30 minutes without oxygen is nothing short of miraculous.

The theme of survival against all odds is vividly portrayed through the physical and environmental challenges faced by Chris. Saturation diving is one of the most perilous professions in the world, and the film underscores the inherent risks of working in such an unforgiving environment. The North Sea, with its crushing pressure, frigid temperatures, and impenetrable darkness, serves as an antagonist in the story; a force of nature that threatens to extinguish life at every turn.

Both the documentary and the feature film emphasize that survival is not just a matter of physical endurance but also mental fortitude. Chris's ability to remain calm under pressure, focus on the slim chance of rescue, and conserve his energy speaks volumes about the human instinct to cling to life. His story reminds viewers that even when hope appears lost, the will to survive can carry us through the most desperate situations.

The filmmakers also explore how survival extends beyond the individual. Chris's ordeal is not just his own battle but one shared by his colleagues and loved ones. Their relentless efforts to rescue him illustrate the interconnectedness of survival, where every life is supported by a network of others working tirelessly behind the scenes.

Human Resilience and Determination

Closely tied to survival is the theme of human resilience; the ability to confront adversity, endure suffering, and emerge stronger. In Last Breath, resilience is shown not only in Chris Lemons but also in his colleagues, who refuse to give up despite the overwhelming odds stacked against them.

For Chris, resilience manifests in his mental discipline and physical strength. While stranded underwater with no communication and diminishing resources, he must confront his fears and rely on his training to increase his chances of survival. The film highlights the mental battle he faces, as isolation and the certainty of death threaten to overwhelm him. Yet, Chris's ability to hold on to hope, however faint, is a testament to the extraordinary resilience of the human spirit.

The story also explores the resilience of the crew aboard the ship. In the face of a crisis, they must work under immense pressure, making split-second decisions and executing complex rescue maneuvers in a high-stakes environment. Their determination to bring Chris back alive, despite the technical challenges and emotional toll, is a powerful example of collective resilience.

Resilience is not just about enduring hardship but also about finding meaning in it. Chris's survival story, and the lessons it imparts, becomes a source of inspiration for others. It demonstrates that even in the most extreme circumstances, human beings are capable of extraordinary feats of strength and perseverance.

Teamwork, Trust, and Camaraderie in High-Risk Professions

One of the most profound themes in Last Breath is the importance of teamwork, trust, and camaraderie in high-risk professions. Saturation diving, by its very nature, requires a deep reliance on others. Divers depend on their colleagues to operate life-support systems, manage emergencies, and execute rescue operations with precision. The story of Chris

Lemons underscores the critical role of trust and teamwork in ensuring survival.

In both the documentary and the feature film, the crew's response to Chris's crisis is a testament to their bond and shared commitment. When Chris becomes stranded underwater, his colleagues immediately spring into action, setting aside their own fears and emotions to focus on the task at hand. The dive supervisor, played by Woody Harrelson in the feature film, exemplifies leadership under pressure, coordinating the rescue efforts and keeping the team focused despite the daunting circumstances.

The film also explores the personal relationships between the crew members, highlighting how camaraderie is forged through shared experiences and mutual reliance. Saturation divers spend weeks at a time in confined spaces, working in one of the most dangerous environments on Earth. This close-knit lifestyle fosters a sense of brotherhood, where each member feels a profound responsibility for the others.

Trust is a recurring motif in the story. Chris trusts his colleagues to do everything in their power to save him, even when communication is lost. Similarly, the crew trusts each other to perform their roles flawlessly under immense pressure. This mutual trust is what makes their rescue operation possible, despite the seemingly impossible odds.

The theme of teamwork extends beyond the professional realm, touching on the emotional connections between the characters. In the feature film, Chris's relationship with his fiancée is given greater emphasis, adding another layer to the story. Her faith in his survival and the emotional support she provides serves as a reminder of the broader network of relationships that sustain individuals in times of crisis.

Universal Lessons from the Story

While Last Breath is rooted in the specific world of saturation diving, its themes have universal resonance. The story of survival, resilience, and teamwork speaks to fundamental aspects of the human experience, making it relatable to audiences from all walks of life.

1. Survival as a Human Instinct: The story reminds us of the innate human drive to survive, even in the face of overwhelming odds. Chris Lemons' ordeal serves as a powerful metaphor for the challenges we all face in life and the importance of never giving up.

2. The Strength of Human Connections: The film highlights the importance of relationships and mutual support in overcoming adversity. Whether it's the bond between colleagues, friends, or loved ones, these connections are what sustain us in difficult times.

3. The Power of Resilience: Chris's ability to endure and survive speaks to the incredible resilience of the human spirit. His story inspires viewers to confront their own challenges with courage and determination.

4. The Value of Teamwork: In high-stakes situations, teamwork and trust are essential. The crew's coordinated efforts to save Chris illustrate the importance of working together toward a common goal, even when the odds seem insurmountable.

The themes of Last Breath; survival, resilience, and teamwork, are what make it a story of enduring significance. Chris Lemons' extraordinary ordeal is not just a tale of personal triumph but a testament to the power of the human spirit and the strength we draw from our connections with others. Whether in the form of the raw and authentic documentary or the dramatized and emotionally charged feature film, Last Breath continues to resonate with audiences, reminding us of what it means to face adversity with courage, hope, and unwavering determination.

Chapter Four

Analysis of the Documentary Last Breath (2019)

The 2019 documentary Last Breath takes audiences on an emotionally intense and gripping journey, chronicling the extraordinary story of saturation diver Chris Lemons and his near-death experience in the North Sea. Directed by Richard da Costa and Alex Parkinson, the documentary uses a combination of real footage, interviews, and expert storytelling techniques to create an immersive and powerful narrative. By blending the harrowing account of Lemons' survival with the personal reflections of those involved, Last Breath stands out as a remarkable example of documentary filmmaking.

Cinematic Techniques and Storytelling Approach
One of the standout aspects of Last Breath is its ability to blend different cinematic techniques to craft a tense, suspenseful, and highly emotional narrative. The filmmakers' approach to telling Chris Lemons' story is marked by the strategic use of pacing, visual style, and narrative structure.

The documentary begins with an urgent and immediate sense of tension. From the outset, the audience is thrust into the extreme conditions of the North Sea, a place that is both beautifully eerie and perilously dangerous. The film's use of pacing is central to maintaining a sense of urgency throughout the story. Early on, there is a constant feeling of impending danger, as the camera lingers on the faces of those involved in the rescue operation, capturing their anxiety and determination. The filmmakers create a sense of claustrophobia, not just by emphasizing the isolated environment in which Chris is trapped but also by showcasing the tight-knit team of divers and crew who must act quickly and efficiently to save him.

The storytelling approach of Last Breath follows a chronological structure that leads up to the climactic rescue operation, before revisiting the aftermath. By piecing together the sequence of events, the documentary builds suspense and draws the audience into Chris's experience in a way that heightens the stakes of the narrative. This linear approach allows viewers to grasp the immense challenges that each person faces; both in the underwater depths and on the surface, as they work together to overcome the odds.

The juxtaposition of interviews and archival footage adds depth to the documentary's storytelling. By interviewing Chris Lemons, his colleagues, and family members, the filmmakers give a personal and emotional insight into the ordeal. These interviews are key in humanizing the story, adding layers of empathy and emotion. The documentary is not just a recounting of events; it is a deep exploration of the emotional toll that such high-risk work takes on the individuals involved. The filmmakers do not shy away from showing the raw, unfiltered emotions of those in the midst of the crisis, capturing their fear, hope, and relief as the story unfolds.

Use of Real Footage and Interviews
The use of real footage is one of the documentary's most powerful techniques, heightening the authenticity and emotional weight of the story. The film incorporates actual footage from the ill-fated dive and the subsequent rescue operation, offering viewers an unvarnished glimpse of the high-stakes profession of saturation diving. These moments are juxtaposed with interviews from Chris and the crew, adding context and insight into the

technical and emotional complexity of the situation.

For instance, the footage of Chris's underwater accident, where a cable becomes tangled, is shown in its raw, unpolished form. This directorial choice places viewers in the heart of the moment, amplifying the fear and desperation of the incident. By using real-time footage, the documentary makes the audience feel like active participants in the event rather than passive observers. It also fosters a deep connection between the audience and the individuals on screen, making their emotions feel more immediate and tangible.

In addition to the underwater footage, the documentary features interviews with key individuals involved in the incident. Chris Lemons speaks candidly about his thoughts, emotions, and physical state during the ordeal, providing first-hand insight into the psychological aspects of the situation. His recollections are powerful and evocative, recounting his struggle to keep calm while running out of air, the physical exhaustion, and his hope for rescue. His words, alongside the visceral footage, offer a deeply personal connection for viewers, making the story all the more heart-wrenching.

Other interviews feature the members of the dive team, who describe the intense pressure they were under to execute the rescue, as well as their emotional response when they realized Chris was alive. These testimonies serve to highlight the camaraderie and trust that exists between colleagues in such high-risk professions. Through these real-life accounts, the documentary explores the human aspects of the story; personal sacrifice, resilience, and the collective effort of a team working against time to save one of their own.

Emotional Impact on the Audience
The emotional impact of Last Breath is undeniably powerful. The documentary is an emotional rollercoaster that effectively takes

viewers through the high stakes of the rescue operation, followed by a sense of deep relief once Chris is brought to safety. The filmmakers create an emotional connection by allowing the audience to witness the personal toll of Chris's ordeal—not just on him, but also on his family, his colleagues, and the people around him.

One of the most moving moments in the film comes when Chris recounts his inner thoughts during the time he was trapped underwater. His sense of isolation and helplessness is palpable, and his words reveal a vulnerability that resonates deeply with the audience. The documentary does not shy away from exploring the mental anguish of being trapped in such dire circumstances. Chris's reflections on his desire to survive for his family, especially his fiancée, strike a particularly emotional chord. His determination to keep fighting for life, despite the odds, serves as a poignant reminder of the resilience of the human spirit.

The film also focuses on the emotional responses of the rescue team. As they work against time to bring Chris back to the surface, their anxiety and fear are laid bare. The stress of such a dangerous profession is made even more intense by the personal connection each member of the team feels toward their colleague. The filmmakers capture these moments with sensitivity, showing that while the divers are highly skilled professionals, they are also deeply human and capable of experiencing fear, doubt, and exhaustion.

Furthermore, the impact of the documentary is amplified by the use of sound and music. The soundtrack complements the visuals, building tension during the most critical moments and providing a sense of relief when Chris is saved. The use of silence during key moments of the ordeal, such as when Chris is running out of air or when the rescue crew is frantically working to retrieve him, creates a haunting effect. This intentional stillness intensifies the emotional weight of the situation, forcing the audience to confront the gravity of what is happening.

Another emotional layer is added through the reflections of Chris's family and fiancée. Their perspectives help convey the personal stakes of the story, making the audience care not only about the outcome of the rescue operation but also about the lives affected by it. The interviews with Chris's loved ones remind viewers that the consequences of such incidents reach far beyond the immediate crisis, and the emotional fallout lingers long after the event has passed.

Last Breath (2019) stands out as an exceptional documentary that combines cinematic techniques, real footage, and heartfelt interviews to tell a gripping, emotional, and ultimately inspiring survival story. Through its innovative storytelling approach, the documentary creates an atmosphere of tension and suspense while also delving into the emotional complexities of human survival. The use of real footage and interviews with those directly involved in the ordeal gives the film a sense of authenticity that enhances its emotional impact.

In the end, Last Breath is more than just a survival story. It is an exploration of the human spirit, the resilience required to overcome insurmountable challenges, and the emotional connections that sustain us through the darkest of moments. The documentary is not just about the physical survival of Chris Lemons—it is about the collective strength of his colleagues, the emotional toll of such high-risk work, and the universal theme of perseverance against all odds. Through its masterful use of cinematic techniques, Last Breath leaves a lasting emotional imprint on its viewers, inviting them to reflect on their own capacity for resilience, empathy, and hope.

Chapter Five

Analysis of the Feature Film Last Breath (2025)

The 2025 feature film Last Breath, directed by Alex Parkinson, is a thrilling and emotional cinematic recreation of the real-life near-death experience of saturation diver Chris Lemons in the North Sea. While the film draws inspiration from the 2019 documentary of the same name,

Parkinson's direction and the performances of a talented cast elevate the story into a dramatic and suspenseful narrative. The film explores the profound emotional and psychological effects of surviving in one of the harshest environments on Earth, the deep ocean, while showcasing human resilience, teamwork, and the fight for survival.

Directorial Vision of Alex Parkinson
Alex Parkinson, best known for his work on documentaries such as Last Breath (2019), brings a unique directorial vision to the feature film adaptation. Parkinson's transition from documentary filmmaking to narrative cinema is seamless, as he retains the authenticity and emotional depth that made the original documentary so impactful. However, as a feature film, he also incorporates elements of suspense, action, and character development that heighten the dramatic stakes of the story.

Parkinson's direction in Last Breath focuses on two key aspects: the visceral experience of underwater diving and the emotional toll of survival. His commitment to authenticity is evident in how he captures the isolating and perilous conditions of saturation diving, ensuring the audience feels the claustrophobia and the life-threatening environment that Chris Lemons navigates. The film doesn't simply present the physical danger of the North Sea; it also delves into the mental and emotional anguish that the characters endure.

In his directorial vision, Parkinson emphasizes the inner turmoil and the fight for survival that define Lemons' experience. The film takes the real-life story of Chris Lemons and expands on the emotional and psychological journey he undergoes while trapped in the deep sea. Parkinson does not shy away from showing the vulnerability of the characters, particularly Lemons, who struggles not just with the physical conditions of being underwater but also with fear, isolation, and the uncertainty of whether he will make it out alive. This is portrayed in a way that invites the audience to reflect on the fragility of human life and the will to survive.

Moreover, Parkinson uses the team-based rescue operation as a central plot element, focusing on the camaraderie, trust, and determination of the individuals working together to save Chris. By weaving together the diver's experience with the teamwork on the surface, Parkinson creates a dynamic narrative that balances high-intensity action with emotional beats, which resonate deeply with the audience.

Performance of the Cast
The cast of Last Breath (2025) is one of its key strengths, with top-tier performances that bring the characters to life and amplify the emotional stakes of the story. The film stars Woody Harrelson, Simu Liu, and Finn Cole in pivotal roles, each of whom delivers a performance that resonates with authenticity and depth.

Woody Harrelson as Captain Mark Taylor
Woody Harrelson's portrayal of Captain Mark Taylor, the leader of the rescue operation, is one

of the standout performances in the film. Taylor is the embodiment of calm under pressure, and Harrelson brings a quiet intensity to the role. Throughout the movie, he plays the character as a seasoned, no-nonsense leader who is deeply committed to saving his colleague. Harrelson's portrayal is grounded in a mixture of professionalism and empathy, making Taylor both a stern authority figure and a compassionate teammate. His ability to convey the weight of the rescue operation without becoming melodramatic adds a sense of realism to the high-stakes situation. Harrelson's performance is one that anchors the narrative, and his character's journey reflects the emotional tension felt by the team as they desperately race against time.

Simu Liu as Chris Lemons
Simu Liu, known for his role in Shang-Chi and the Legend of the Ten Rings, takes on the role of Chris Lemons, the diver who faces a life-threatening ordeal deep in the North Sea. Liu brings a combination of vulnerability,

determination, and physicality to the role. As Chris Lemons, Liu portrays a man who must come to terms with his fear and isolation while also maintaining a focus on survival. His performance captures the internal conflict of a man fighting for his life, both mentally and physically. Liu's ability to convey the emotional turmoil of being trapped underwater—facing the physical constraints of diving while grappling with his mounting fear—adds a profound emotional layer to the character. He conveys Chris' sense of helplessness, yet also his quiet strength, and ultimately his resolve to survive. Liu's performance allows the audience to connect with Chris on a deeply personal level, making the stakes of the story even more intense.

Finn Cole as Matt, the Rescue Diver
Finn Cole plays Matt, a key member of the rescue team tasked with saving Chris Lemons. Cole brings a sense of urgency and determination to the role, portraying a young diver who is pushed to his limits as he navigates

the complex and perilous conditions of the North Sea. Matt's character is vital to the narrative, as he symbolizes the team-based efforts to bring Chris back to safety. Cole's performance as Matt is marked by a mixture of raw emotion and technical expertise, showing the physical and emotional strain of the rescue operation. His performance makes the audience feel the weight of the decisions being made and the challenges faced by the divers, contributing significantly to the tension and emotional impact of the film.

The ensemble cast also includes supporting roles that help create a dynamic and compelling group of characters. The performances of the supporting cast members further highlight the themes of teamwork and resilience, demonstrating that each individual involved in the rescue operation plays a crucial role in ensuring Chris's survival.

Visual and Sound Effects in Recreating the Underwater Environment

diving, serve to heighten the tension of each scene. The sound of bubbles escaping, the constant hum of the diving equipment, and the ominous background noise of the ocean's currents all add to the realism of the underwater sequences.

Moreover, the sound design contrasts the stillness of the underwater environment with the urgency of the rescue operation on the surface. The sound of radio transmissions, the equipment being moved, and the voices of the rescuers communicating add to the sense of chaos and pressure. The sound effects, paired with the visual elements, make the audience feel as though they are right there with Chris, trapped in the depths, as well as with the rescue team, who must work together to save him.

Last Breath (2025) is a powerful and immersive feature film that successfully builds on the real-life events of the 2019 documentary. Director Alex Parkinson's vision, combined with exceptional performances from Woody

Harrelson, Simu Liu, Finn Cole, and the supporting cast, creates a captivating narrative of survival, teamwork, and human resilience. The visual and sound effects, particularly in recreating the underwater environment, enhance the film's intensity and emotional impact, drawing the audience into the high-stakes situation. The feature film adaptation of Last Breath not only honors the real-life story but also elevates it to a dramatic and thrilling cinematic experience. Through its direction, performances, and technical achievements, the film successfully captures the tension, fear, and hope that defined Chris Lemons' miraculous survival.

Chapter Six

Comparative Review: Documentary vs. Feature Film; Last Breath (2019 vs. 2025)

The real-life survival story of saturation diver Chris Lemons, trapped in the depths of the North Sea, is both extraordinary and emotionally gripping. The story has been adapted into two distinct forms: the 2019 documentary Last Breath and the 2025 feature film Last Breath. Both versions aim to tell the harrowing story of Lemons' struggle for survival after a life-threatening accident during a routine dive. However, the two adaptations; while rooted in the same real events, differ in their approach, tone, and method of storytelling.

Authenticity and Accuracy in Both Versions

The Documentary (2019)
As a documentary, Last Breath (2019) is committed to presenting an unfiltered, factual account of Chris Lemons' ordeal in the North Sea. The film uses real footage, interviews with the people involved in the incident, and firsthand accounts to convey the gravity of the situation. The documentary relies heavily on the real-life

voices and perspectives of the rescue team, family members, and Chris himself. Through these personal testimonies, the film captures the emotional depth of the story while maintaining the authenticity of the event.

One of the strengths of the documentary is its adherence to realism. By using actual footage of Chris' recovery and interviews with the people who were there during the rescue, the documentary avoids any sensationalism or dramatic embellishments. This lends the film a sense of veracity that is often lacking in dramatized portrayals. Viewers are able to hear directly from Chris about his physical and mental state during the ordeal, as well as from the rescue team, giving the audience an inside look at the real-life challenges faced by both the diver and the people working to bring him back to the surface.

However, the documentary's emphasis on factual accuracy also means it forgoes some of the emotional impact that a narrative film might provide. The real-time nature of the footage and the interviews, while informative, can at times feel disconnected, as they often lack the tension and dramatic pacing necessary to pull the audience into the moment. While the documentary is powerful in its rawness, it does not delve as deeply into character development or the psychological journey of the individuals involved, something that a feature film can explore more fully.

The Feature Film (2025)
In contrast, the 2025 feature film Last Breath takes liberties with the source material in order to deliver a more dramatized and emotional narrative. While it retains the core of the real-life events, the film introduces fictionalized elements, including fictionalized dialogue, additional characters, and extended narrative arcs that flesh out the characters' personal stories. This allows the film to explore themes like human resilience, fear, and hope in a more immersive and emotionally charged way.

The accuracy of the feature film is somewhat compromised by the need to create dramatic tension and to engage the audience on an emotional level. The depiction of underwater scenes, for example, is visually stunning, but at times the film exaggerates the physical peril and the emotional intensity of the situation in ways that the documentary does not. While the film captures the essence of Chris Lemons' experience, it does so with heightened stakes and a more cinematic sensibility. The use of creative license in the film helps to make the story more accessible to a broader audience, but it risks distorting the reality of the events.

Strengths and Weaknesses of the Adaptations

Strengths of the Documentary

The primary strength of the documentary lies in its authenticity. By relying on real footage and firsthand accounts, Last Breath (2019) offers a raw and unembellished look at the events surrounding Chris Lemons' survival. The interviews with Chris, his colleagues, and the rescue team offer an unparalleled level of insight into the emotional and psychological toll of the ordeal. The documentary emphasizes the gravity of the situation without resorting to melodrama, which gives it a powerful emotional weight that feels grounded in reality.

Another strength is the pacing and focus of the documentary. As it chronicles the events in a linear, fact-based manner, the audience is taken through the incident step-by-step. This gives the viewer a deeper understanding of the rescue operation's complexity, as well as the painstaking effort it took to reach Chris. The documentary also benefits from a more immersive focus on the technical aspects of saturation diving, providing an educational perspective that deepens the audience's understanding of the risks involved in the profession.

Weaknesses of the Documentary
While the documentary's commitment to realism is its strength, it also becomes a limitation. The storytelling can feel somewhat disjointed at

times, as the film shifts between interviews, archival footage, and narration. While this approach creates a sense of objectivity, it lacks the emotional resonance that is often needed to engage a wider audience. Additionally, the film is somewhat clinical in its approach, providing details about the dive and the rescue operation but not delving deeply enough into the emotional journey of the key individuals involved. The absence of dramatization limits the potential for audience connection, especially for viewers unfamiliar with the technicalities of saturation diving or the context of the rescue.

Strengths of the Feature Film
The feature film's greatest strength is its ability to dramatize the emotional and psychological aspects of the story. By adding depth to the characters and dramatizing the events, Last Breath (2025) creates a narrative that is emotionally gripping and suspenseful. The performances of the cast, including Woody Harrelson, Simu Liu, and Finn Cole, help to bring the characters' personal struggles to life,

particularly Chris Lemons' internal battle for survival. The film's pacing, with carefully timed action sequences and quieter moments of reflection, draws the audience deeper into the experience.

The cinematic techniques in the film, such as the stunning underwater visuals and intense sound design, also elevate the impact of the story. The feature film's ability to immerse the audience in the harsh and unforgiving environment of the North Sea makes it a visually compelling experience. The underwater sequences are crafted with such precision and artistry that the audience can feel the weight of the water, the isolation, and the constant threat of danger.

Weaknesses of the Feature Film
While the feature film excels in emotional storytelling, it risks losing some of the authenticity of the real-life events. The dramatization, while effective in heightening the emotional stakes, occasionally veers into exaggeration. The portrayal of Chris Lemons'

struggle, for example, is more intense and action-packed than what the documentary presents. This is not necessarily a weakness in itself but is a departure from the grounded realism of the documentary. The fictionalized aspects, such as added character development and expanded dialogue, can sometimes detract from the raw emotional impact of the real events.

Another potential weakness is the simplified portrayal of some of the more technical aspects of saturation diving. While the film does convey the general risks involved, it sacrifices some of the complexity of the real-world diving operations in favor of making the story more accessible to a mainstream audience. This makes the film less educational than the documentary, and it may leave viewers with less of an understanding of the dangerous nature of the profession.

Impact of Dramatization vs. Realism

The impact of dramatization versus realism is a key point of contrast between the documentary and the feature film. The documentary's reliance on real footage and interviews brings an undeniable authenticity to the story, allowing the audience to engage with the raw emotion of the events without any embellishment. This realism gives the audience a deeper appreciation for the complexities of saturation diving and the dangers faced by Chris Lemons and his colleagues. However, this focus on realism can be emotionally distancing, as it does not provide the same kind of cinematic engagement that a feature film offers.

In contrast, the feature film's dramatization provides a heightened emotional experience that draws the audience in. The intense performances, the dramatic pacing, and the powerful visuals make it more accessible to a broader audience. However, the dramatization risks oversimplifying or exaggerating the real-life events, which may result in a loss of the story's true essence for some viewers.

Both the documentary Last Breath (2019) and the feature film adaptation (2025) offer compelling portrayals of Chris Lemons' extraordinary survival story. The documentary excels in its authenticity and factual accuracy, providing an immersive, real-world perspective on the incident. The feature film, meanwhile, delivers an emotionally intense and visually stunning narrative that highlights the human struggle for survival. While the documentary stays true to the rawness of the real events, the feature film introduces dramatization to create a more visceral cinematic experience. Ultimately, the choice between the two versions depends on the viewer's preference for realism versus emotional engagement. Both adaptations succeed in honoring the story of Chris Lemons, albeit in different ways, and both leave a lasting impact on their audience.

Chapter Seven

Character Exploration; Last Breath (2019 Documentary vs. 2025 Feature Film)

The story of Chris Lemons, a saturation diver who faced a near-death experience in the North Sea, is one of survival, resilience, and hope. His harrowing experience, which saw him trapped at the bottom of the sea for over three hours with only a limited oxygen supply, became the focal point of the documentary Last Breath (2019) and the feature film adaptation Last Breath (2025). While both adaptations center around the core events of Lemons' survival, they each present his character in different lights. The documentary stays grounded in the real-life person, while the feature film offers a dramatized version of the man, with an emphasis on human emotion, cinematic storytelling, and artistic license. Alongside Chris, the supporting characters; his fellow divers, the rescue team, and his family, play an equally vital role in both versions of the story, emphasizing the importance of teamwork, trust, and determination in overcoming adversity. In this character exploration, we will compare the portrayal of Chris Lemons across both versions and examine the significance of the supporting characters in the context of the larger narrative of survival.

Chris Lemons: Real-Life Hero vs. On-Screen Portrayal

The Documentary (2019)

In the documentary Last Breath (2019), Chris Lemons is presented as a real-life hero who displays incredible mental and physical fortitude in the face of overwhelming odds. As the central figure of the story, his character is grounded in the raw reality of the situation. The documentary allows the audience to hear directly from Chris about his emotions and state of mind during the incident, presenting his thoughts in an unfiltered manner. This approach gives the viewer a direct connection with Lemons' experience, allowing them to understand the harrowing physical toll, as well as the deep psychological struggle he faced while being trapped underwater with only a dwindling supply of oxygen.

One of the key aspects of Chris' real-life portrayal in the documentary is his calmness and determination in the face of an excruciatingly dangerous situation. His calm voice, though occasionally strained, offers insight into his mental resolve. As he recounts the events of the night, the audience becomes aware of his internal battle between survival instincts and the inevitability of death. The documentary focuses heavily on Chris' own recollections, using these intimate moments to depict his personal strength, determination, and the moments of doubt and fear he had to overcome. The audience gains a real sense of who Chris is beyond his heroic survival story; he is portrayed as a professional diver, a family man, and an individual who has faced incredible hardship with stoic resolve.

The Feature Film (2025)
In the 2025 feature film Last Breath, Chris Lemons' character is given a more fleshed-out, dramatized narrative. Played by Finn Cole, Chris is portrayed as a man who struggles with the weight of his job, his relationship with his

colleagues, and the overwhelming responsibility that comes with working in one of the most dangerous professions. The film takes creative liberties, adding personal backstory and character arcs that do not appear in the documentary. For example, the film introduces scenes where Chris grapples with his emotional vulnerabilities, such as his feelings of isolation and his relationship with his wife. These elements deepen his characterization and add dramatic tension to the narrative.

One of the most significant differences between the real-life and on-screen portrayals is the heightened sense of inner turmoil and emotional conflict that the film introduces. In the documentary, Chris comes across as a steady and composed figure. In contrast, the feature film portrays him as a more conflicted, anxious man who doubts his survival, questioning whether he can hold on long enough to be saved. These dramatized moments provide a more emotional journey for the audience, enabling them to empathize with the character's vulnerability in ways the documentary may not have fully captured.

However, while the feature film version of Chris may be more emotionally expressive, this dramatization risks losing some of the quiet dignity and stoicism that characterize the real-life Chris Lemons. The real-life heroism of Chris, as presented in the documentary, shines through his calmness in a life-threatening situation. In contrast, the feature film leans more into the emotional highs and lows, providing a more cinematic experience, but one that feels less restrained and perhaps less faithful to the true essence of his character.

Supporting Characters and Their Significance

The Documentary (2019)
In the documentary, the supporting characters are drawn primarily from Chris' real-life rescue

team, including his colleagues in the diving operation, the emergency personnel involved in the rescue, and his family members. These characters play a crucial role in underscoring the team-oriented nature of saturation diving and the rescue operation. The film focuses on how each member of the team contributed to Chris' survival, as well as the personal stakes and relationships involved.

The rescue team's role is portrayed with an emphasis on the gravity of their job. Chris' fellow divers and colleagues back on land are shown working tirelessly to retrieve him from the depths. The documentary highlights the complexity and precision required in a saturation diving operation, showcasing the teamwork and coordination necessary to carry out such a high-risk rescue. The team's collective dedication to Chris' survival, coupled with the technical expertise involved in saturation diving, is central to the success of the operation.

Chris' family, particularly his wife, also features prominently in the documentary. While their inclusion is brief, their emotional responses to the situation help to humanize Chris and offer a broader perspective on the impact of such dangerous work. The emotional toll on his wife, who must cope with the uncertainty of his survival, provides a poignant counterpoint to the physical danger of the underwater environment.

The Feature Film (2025)
In the 2025 feature film, the supporting characters are more fleshed out, with added backstories and interpersonal dynamics that serve to heighten the emotional stakes. Woody Harrelson plays the role of the experienced diver and mentor to Chris, while Simu Liu portrays a younger, more eager member of the team. These characters are developed to create a contrast with Chris, highlighting themes of mentorship, teamwork, and the generational divide within high-risk professions.

The supporting cast also includes fictionalized versions of Chris' family members. The film explores the emotional impact of Chris' job on his personal life, particularly the tension between his work and his relationship with his wife. The addition of these personal dynamics helps to humanize Chris and adds dramatic depth to the narrative. However, while these characters enhance the emotional resonance of the film, they do not fully reflect the real-life people who were involved in Chris' rescue.

The inclusion of fictionalized backstories for these supporting characters serves to create more personal stakes in the story. It allows the film to delve deeper into the interpersonal relationships that may have influenced the outcome of the rescue, but at the cost of accuracy to the real-life individuals involved.

Role of Teamwork in the Story

The Documentary (2019)

In both the documentary and the feature film, teamwork is a central theme. The documentary portrays the success of the rescue as a collective effort, with Chris' survival ultimately being the result of the synchronized work of his colleagues, the rescue team, and the support crew. The documentary emphasizes the technical collaboration between divers, as well as the emotional and moral support that the team provided Chris. It also underscores the physical challenges the rescuers faced, from the difficult underwater conditions to the complex and hazardous nature of saturation diving.

The theme of teamwork is depicted in its most essential form: a professional, mission-focused collaboration where everyone works toward a common goal. There are no unnecessary distractions; just a focused, determined effort to bring Chris home. This highlights the professionalism and dedication of the team, and serves as a reminder of the real risks that saturation divers face every day.

The Feature Film (2025)

In the feature film, the importance of teamwork is also a central theme, but it is portrayed with a greater emotional emphasis. The dynamics between Chris, his mentor, and the rest of the team are given more attention, and the film delves into the relationships between the characters as they face the life-threatening crisis. The teamwork in the film is not just about professional duty; it is about personal sacrifice, trust, and overcoming internal conflicts to achieve a common goal. The film's portrayal of the rescue emphasizes the emotional weight of these relationships, making the audience more invested in the well-being of each character.

The emotional stakes are heightened by the film's narrative choices, which focus on how the characters' personal struggles intertwine with their professional roles. These additional emotional beats provide a more dramatic and compelling narrative, but they also move away from the factual, professional teamwork portrayed in the documentary.

In both Last Breath (2019) and Last Breath (2025), Chris Lemons is presented as a figure of immense resilience and strength, though the adaptations portray him in different lights. The documentary presents him as a stoic hero who survives through sheer mental resolve, while the feature film adds emotional depth to his character by exploring his personal struggles and vulnerabilities. The supporting characters, including the rescue team and Chris' family, play vital roles in both versions, with the documentary focusing on their technical expertise and the feature film emphasizing emotional dynamics. Ultimately, the story of Last Breath showcases the power of teamwork in extreme circumstances, but the portrayal of that teamwork differs depending on the medium; realistic and technical in the documentary, emotional and dramatic in the feature film. Both versions offer valuable insights into the human spirit, but they do so in unique ways.

Last Breath:A Tale of Survival in the Depths

Chapter Eight

Cinematography and Visual Style; Last Breath (2019 Documentary vs. 2025 Feature Film)

The cinematography and visual style in both the 2019 documentary Last Breath and the 2025 feature film Last Breath play an essential role in immersing the audience into the intense world of saturation diving and the harrowing rescue mission of Chris Lemons. Both versions use a combination of innovative underwater filming techniques, strategic lighting, and sound design to evoke the tension, danger, and emotional stakes of the story. While the documentary employs real footage to create an authentic, raw visual experience, the feature film uses cinematic techniques and visual effects to heighten the drama and immerse viewers in the dangerous underwater world.

In this chapter, we will explore how the cinematography and visual style differ between the documentary and the feature film, particularly with regard to underwater filming techniques, the use of lighting and sound design, and the depiction of deep-sea dangers. By examining these elements, we can gain a deeper understanding of how each version conveys the themes of survival, resilience, and teamwork, and how visual style contributes to the emotional experience of the audience.

Underwater Filming Techniques

The Documentary (2019)
In Last Breath (2019), the underwater footage is one of the most striking aspects of the documentary's cinematography. The documentary uses real, unaltered footage captured from the actual saturation diving operation that Chris Lemons was a part of, alongside carefully selected interviews and archival material. The underwater scenes are filmed using specialized camera equipment,

providing an authentic and raw portrayal of the underwater environment where the incident took place. The documentary includes scenes shot from the perspective of the divers themselves, creating a sense of immediacy and realism that enhances the audience's connection to the events. This immersive technique allows viewers to experience the disorienting and perilous conditions of deep-sea diving as if they were part of the rescue team.

The decision to use actual footage brings with it a level of authenticity that adds to the overall tension and realism of the story. The underwater shots are often murky, dark, and difficult to navigate, reflecting the treacherous environment in which Chris Lemons found himself. The limited visibility and confined spaces are portrayed with brutal honesty, underscoring the dangers inherent in the job of saturation divers. The documentary does not rely on visual spectacle; instead, it uses the rawness of the real footage to convey the immense peril the divers face, creating a sense of palpable danger for the audience.

The Feature Film (2025)
In the 2025 feature film Last Breath, the underwater scenes are recreated using high-end cinematography techniques and visual effects. While the film still seeks to maintain a realistic portrayal of the deep-sea environment, the approach is more controlled, designed to create a heightened visual experience for the audience. The use of visual effects allows the filmmakers to craft the underwater world with precision, adding cinematic flourishes that were not possible with the documentary's real-life footage. The film relies on a mixture of practical underwater shots and CGI to enhance the visuals, especially when depicting Chris' entrapment at the ocean floor and the increasingly perilous conditions.

One notable difference in the feature film's underwater filming is the use of color grading. The filmmakers have chosen to enhance the underwater environment with deep blues and shadowy greens, making the water appear colder and more oppressive. The use of lighting effects creates more dramatic contrasts between light and dark, heightening the tension in the scenes. While this approach is visually stunning, it moves away from the rawness and immediacy of the documentary's realism, providing a more stylized portrayal of the underwater world. These techniques make the underwater sequences visually striking but add an element of artifice that is not present in the documentary's straightforward approach.

Use of Lighting and Sound Design for Tension and Immersion

The Documentary (2019)

The lighting and sound design in the documentary Last Breath play a critical role in creating a sense of tension and immersion. Given that the footage is taken from actual underwater operations, the lighting is naturally constrained by the limitations of the environment. There are no extravagant light sources illuminating the underwater space; instead, the dim, murky waters reflect the oppressive and uncertain conditions faced by the divers. The light, often coming from the diver's headlamps or emergency beacons, serves to highlight the small, confined space of the dive environment. This minimal lighting effectively conveys the sense of isolation and claustrophobia that the divers feel when they are submerged deep beneath the sea.

The sound design in the documentary is similarly understated, but it plays a crucial role in amplifying the tension and immersing the viewer in the experience. The sounds of bubbles, heavy breathing, and mechanical noises from the diving equipment heighten the feeling of being submerged in a dangerous and suffocating environment. The quiet sounds of the diver's breathing, amplified by the underwater microphone, evoke a sense of vulnerability, amplifying the tension of the rescue mission. Additionally, the real-time interviews with Chris

Lemons and other members of the rescue team help build an emotional connection with the viewer, offering a soundscape that blends the sounds of the deep with the voices of the survivors.

Because the documentary relies heavily on real footage and interviews, the lighting and sound design work in tandem to maintain the raw, authentic feel of the story. Every subtle sound and dim light serves to draw the audience deeper into the diver's world, making the story's emotional impact even more powerful.

The Feature Film (2025)
The feature film Last Breath (2025) adopts a more stylized approach to lighting and sound, using these elements to build tension and create a more immersive cinematic experience. The underwater sequences in the film are often bathed in shadows, with beams of light penetrating through the water to create dramatic effects. This use of lighting not only adds visual spectacle but also serves to accentuate the

vastness and danger of the ocean environment. The stark contrast between light and shadow mirrors Chris Lemons' struggle to survive in an unknown and hostile environment. The filmmakers also use lighting to indicate moments of hope and despair, with soft, ethereal light occasionally cutting through the darkness when Chris is on the verge of being rescued.

Sound design plays a similarly crucial role in the film's tension-building techniques. The film uses a mix of natural sound and orchestral score to enhance the emotional depth of the story. While the documentary relied on the sounds of bubbles and breathing to create a sense of immediacy, the feature film builds a more expansive soundscape that emphasizes the isolation and desperation of the situation. The sound of Chris' oxygen tank running low, combined with the overwhelming silence of the deep sea, is amplified in the film, pushing the viewer to experience the same sense of panic and suffocation that Chris feels.

One notable aspect of the film's sound design is the use of a more pronounced musical score, especially during moments of high tension or hope. The score swells in intensity during key moments, often mirroring the emotional peaks and valleys of Chris' journey. While this adds an emotional layer to the story, it also takes the viewer out of the grounded, real-life feel of the documentary, creating a more cinematic, stylized experience.

Visual Realism in Portraying Deep-Sea Dangers

The Documentary (2019)
The documentary Last Breath does an excellent job of depicting the harsh realities of deep-sea diving and the dangers involved in such operations. The visual realism is underscored by the use of actual footage and the absence of high-tech visual effects. The rawness of the imagery emphasizes the unforgiving nature of the deep sea, with murky waters and minimal visibility creating an atmosphere of peril and

uncertainty. The viewers witness the real-life dangers faced by Chris Lemons and his team, including the threat of equipment failure, the physical and psychological toll of working in the depths, and the constant fight against time.

This unfiltered approach to visual realism heightens the tension, as the audience feels the same vulnerability and danger that the divers experience. The documentary doesn't rely on sensationalism or dramatic visuals to convey the stakes; it uses the reality of the situation to create a deeply unsettling experience. The authenticity of the visuals enhances the emotional impact of the film, allowing viewers to witness the true risks of saturation diving firsthand.

The Feature Film (2025)
In contrast, the feature film Last Breath (2025) uses a combination of real underwater sequences and CGI to create a more dramatic and visually spectacular version of the deep-sea dangers. The filmmakers amplify the physical and psychological threats of the environment through

heightened visuals, using special effects to depict Chris Lemons' descent into darkness and his desperate struggle for survival. While the use of CGI allows the filmmakers to create a more polished and visually arresting underwater world, it also removes some of the gritty realism that the documentary captured. The dangers are exaggerated for cinematic effect, making the stakes feel higher than they might have in real life.

However, this visual embellishment works within the context of the feature film, as it serves to heighten the emotional drama of Chris' ordeal. The stark contrasts between light and dark, combined with the visual effects, immerse the audience in the dangerous and mysterious world beneath the waves. The film's depiction of deep-sea dangers is not necessarily more realistic, but it is more visually striking and emotionally charged, reflecting the narrative's heightened drama.

Both Last Breath (2019) and Last Breath (2025) use cinematography and visual style to immerse the audience in the intense and perilous world of saturation diving. The documentary relies on real footage and minimalist techniques to create a raw, authentic experience, using underwater filming, lighting, and sound design to highlight the danger and isolation faced by Chris Lemons. In contrast, the feature film uses a more stylized approach, incorporating CGI, dramatic lighting, and an expansive soundscape to amplify the tension and emotional stakes of the story. Both approaches are effective in their respective contexts, but they offer different viewing experiences; one grounded in realism and the other heightened for cinematic effect. Regardless of the approach, both films succeed in drawing viewers into the terrifying world of the deep sea, emphasizing the life-and-death stakes of survival.

Chapter Nine

Emotional and Psychological Impact; Last Breath (2019 Documentary vs. 2025 Feature Film)

The emotional and psychological impact of Last Breath, both the 2019 documentary and the 2025 feature film, is profound and enduring. Both versions of the story draw on the harrowing real-life experience of saturation diver Chris Lemons, who faced unimaginable challenges after a tragic accident left him trapped on the ocean floor with no power, no communication, and no hope of rescue. The way both films handle the emotional and psychological aspects of this survival story varies significantly, with the documentary taking a more intimate, raw approach and the feature film intensifying the psychological pressure with cinematic techniques. However, both films succeed in creating an atmosphere of intense suspense, isolation, and fear, and each version evokes powerful audience reactions that resonate long after the credits roll.

How the Movie Builds Tension and Suspense

The Documentary (2019)
In the 2019 documentary Last Breath, the tension is built primarily through the pacing of the narrative, the use of real-time footage, and the emotional weight of the survivors' testimonies. The documentary takes a patient, methodical approach to storytelling, allowing the audience to gradually absorb the danger and severity of Chris Lemons' situation. The buildup of suspense is deliberate, as the viewer is kept on edge, unsure whether Chris will survive or not.

The documentary effectively uses interviews with Chris and other key members of the rescue team to add depth to the narrative. The survivors speak in real, unvarnished terms about the horrors of the incident, describing the uncertainty and terror that they felt. These firsthand accounts amplify the emotional tension, and the documentary's decision to focus on the immediacy of the diver's voice; often punctuated by moments of silence, builds a palpable sense of dread.

Moreover, the real-time footage from the dive site plays a crucial role in sustaining the suspense. The camera follows the action from multiple perspectives, including the underwater footage, the view from the surface, and the control rooms, providing a multifaceted approach to the crisis. This immersive perspective allows the audience to feel as if they are right there with Chris and the rescue team, witnessing the stakes grow higher with each passing moment. By avoiding embellishments or fictionalized elements, the documentary builds a raw, unrelenting tension, with the audience acutely aware of the very real risks at play.

The Feature Film (2025)
In contrast, the 2025 feature film Last Breath heightens the tension with a more cinematic approach, employing techniques such as music,

sound design, dramatic lighting, and the use of visual effects to amplify the stakes. The suspense is escalated through the use of sharp editing and the manipulation of the audience's emotional expectations. The filmmakers utilize suspenseful music that rises in pitch, with haunting, eerie tones accompanying the most tense moments, enhancing the anxiety that the audience feels. As Chris' situation becomes increasingly dire, the music swells, increasing the emotional stakes and pushing the viewer into a heightened state of anticipation.

The feature film also intensifies the action through visual effects and heightened dramatic sequences. For example, the physical dangers of the underwater environment; such as the risk of the diving equipment failing, the danger of being lost in the deep, and the psychological effects of isolation; are often underscored by rapid cuts and a dynamic camera that mirrors the escalating panic of the characters. The use of lighting, particularly the contrast between the dark, suffocating waters and the occasional shafts of light piercing the surface, adds to the sense of impending doom. The filmmakers take creative liberties in dramatizing Chris' struggle to survive, keeping the audience on edge through visual and auditory cues that heighten the emotional impact.

Both the documentary and feature film use time as an element of suspense, but the feature film uses its more stylized and exaggerated pacing to create a more pressing sense of urgency. By breaking up the narrative with action sequences and emotional beats, the film ensures that the tension never fully dissipates, constantly re-engaging the audience's emotions.

Depiction of Isolation and Fear

The Documentary (2019)
One of the most striking emotional and psychological elements of Last Breath (2019) is the depiction of isolation. Chris Lemons, trapped on the ocean floor with no way of communicating with the surface, faces a deep

psychological battle. The documentary takes an unflinching approach to this isolation, focusing on the eerie silence of the ocean, the disorienting darkness, and the claustrophobia of being confined in a submerged metal cage. With minimal communication between Chris and his team, the viewer feels the crushing loneliness of his predicament. This sense of isolation is also heightened by the calm, measured tone of the documentary's narration, which contrasts sharply with the underlying sense of panic in the diver's situation.

The fear that Chris Lemons experiences in these moments is palpable, but the documentary does not overemphasize the emotion. Instead, it subtly conveys the terror through the silence, the broken communication, and the stark reality of what was happening. The filmmakers allow Chris' voice to shine through, providing the audience with a raw, unfiltered account of his experience. This directness, without dramatic embellishments, forces the audience to confront the visceral fear of being trapped in an environment so hostile and so far removed from help.

The documentary doesn't shy away from depicting Chris' vulnerability, and the interviews with those involved in the rescue mission provide a window into the emotional toll it took on both Chris and the rescue team. The stress and fear are palpable as the rescue workers are faced with the overwhelming task of saving him.

The Feature Film (2025)
The feature film Last Breath (2025) takes the themes of isolation and fear and amplifies them for dramatic effect. In the film, Chris' experience of being trapped on the ocean floor is filled with heightened emotional intensity. The audience is given a more visceral, cinematic portrayal of the physical and psychological toll isolation takes on Chris. His fear is depicted not just through his thoughts and emotions but also through physical symptoms: hyperventilation, disorientation, and despair. The film's pacing allows for more moments of psychological

exploration, giving us a deeper look at Chris' mental state as he grapples with the fear of not being rescued.

The underwater environment is depicted as a vast, suffocating void, with the darkness becoming a near-constant presence. The feature film uses visuals to emphasize the profound isolation Chris faces—loneliness is conveyed not only through Chris' dialogue but also through the solitary visuals of his environment. The underwater shots show him floating in the emptiness, with an overwhelming sense of scale that emphasizes the size of the ocean and the smallness of the human form against it.

This isolation is heightened by the use of sound design, as the constant hum of underwater machinery, the rhythmic breathing of the divers, and the absence of communication serve to isolate Chris even more. The muffled, oppressive sounds mirror the psychological state of the character, heightening the tension in every scene.

Audience Reactions and Takeaways

The Documentary (2019)
The documentary Last Breath evokes strong emotional reactions from its audience, primarily because of its raw, unembellished portrayal of a true-life crisis. Viewers are drawn into the narrative not by high-octane action but by the slow-building tension, the humanity of the characters involved, and the emotional honesty of the interviews. The viewer experiences a sense of empathy and helplessness as they are confronted with the stark reality of Chris Lemons' situation. Many viewers are left with a sense of awe at the resilience and survival instinct that allowed Chris to endure such an extraordinary challenge.

The documentary leaves its audience with lingering questions about the nature of survival in extreme situations and the psychological resilience required to confront death head-on. It provides an authentic reflection on human vulnerability, and many viewers come away with a greater respect for the risks faced by those who work in high-risk professions.

The Feature Film (2025)
In contrast, the feature film Last Breath elicits a different emotional reaction, fueled by its heightened dramatic elements. The visual spectacle, the soundtrack, and the emotional performances work together to create a more intense, sometimes overwhelming experience for the audience. Viewers may feel more emotionally charged by the stylized portrayal of Chris' struggle and may experience a heightened sense of relief or catharsis when he is finally rescued. The film may inspire awe at the technical marvels of deep-sea diving and human perseverance, but it may also leave viewers reflecting on the broader themes of teamwork, isolation, and the fear of facing death in such a hostile environment.

The emotional intensity of the film often leaves the audience pondering the psychological toll of such extreme circumstances. For many viewers, the film amplifies the concept of survival, asking what it means to endure against seemingly insurmountable odds.

Both the 2019 documentary and the 2025 feature film Last Breath deeply explore the emotional and psychological impact of isolation, fear, and survival. While the documentary takes a raw, authentic approach, allowing the true story to unfold with minimal embellishment, the feature film heightens the tension, fear, and emotional stakes with cinematic techniques. Both versions masterfully convey the profound psychological and emotional experience of Chris Lemons, drawing the audience into his world with empathy, suspense, and a lasting impact. Whether through the emotional honesty of the documentary or the dramatic flourishes of the feature film, both versions leave audiences with a deeper understanding of human resilience and the lengths to which people will go to survive in the most desperate circumstances.

Chapter Ten

Lessons and Takeaways from Last Breath (2019 Documentary & 2025 Feature Film)

Last Breath, whether in its 2019 documentary form or 2025 feature film adaptation, offers powerful lessons and takeaways, providing insights not just into the dangerous world of deep-sea diving and high-risk professions but also into the broader reflections on life, survival, and human resilience. Through the harrowing real-life experience of Chris Lemons, both versions of the story emphasize the importance of safety, teamwork, and the profound psychological and emotional challenges faced by individuals in extreme conditions. These lessons transcend the specific context of deep-sea diving and resonate with many aspects of human endeavor, making Last Breath an educational and thought-provoking exploration of risk, survival, and the human spirit.

Insights into Deep-Sea Diving and High-Risk Professions

The Dangers and Realities of Deep-Sea Diving
Deep-sea diving, particularly saturation diving as depicted in Last Breath, is one of the most dangerous and high-risk professions in the world. The film and documentary provide an up-close look at the harrowing conditions these divers face. Saturation diving involves staying at depths of up to 1,000 feet for extended periods, often for weeks, with divers living in pressurized chambers before diving. This environment exposes them to dangers such as decompression sickness, equipment failure, underwater currents, and the isolation of being far removed from any immediate help. The lack of immediate escape or rescue options makes the profession especially perilous.

Through Chris Lemons' ordeal, the audience gains a better understanding of the vulnerability these divers face. In his case, a tragic accident caused a complete power failure, plunging his underwater dive site into complete darkness, and leaving him stranded with no way to communicate with his team. This moment highlights the unpredictability of deep-sea diving and the thin line between life and death that divers constantly walk. The sheer unpredictability of the underwater world, where everything can change in an instant, offers a sobering reminder of the risks these professionals face daily.

In both the documentary and feature film, viewers also see the extensive training, technology, and safety measures divers use to mitigate risks. For instance, the divers undergo rigorous training in underwater navigation, emergency procedures, and the management of complex diving equipment. The films underscore how essential it is for divers to trust their gear, their training, and their team to survive these extreme environments. The portrayal of saturation diving emphasizes that it's not just the physical endurance required but also the mental and emotional resilience that's necessary to succeed in such a high-stakes environment.

High-Risk Professions Beyond Diving

Though Last Breath focuses specifically on the world of deep-sea diving, the broader lessons of working in high-risk professions are universal. Many fields; whether in law enforcement, firefighting, military service, or other critical industries, demand similar levels of preparation, courage, and resilience. Just as saturation divers rely on their ability to remain calm under pressure, professionals in these other high-risk fields face life-or-death decisions daily. The movie allows viewers to appreciate the importance of not just the technical aspects of such jobs but the emotional and psychological fortitude required to make life-saving decisions in moments of crisis.

The dedication and discipline that professionals in high-risk fields must have are laid bare in Last Breath. The story of Chris Lemons' survival hinges on a network of support, technology, and expertise, all of which work in tandem to save him. While the focus is on the diver, it becomes clear that the success of high-risk operations involves collaboration between numerous individuals, each bringing specialized knowledge and skill to the table.

Importance of Safety Protocols and Teamwork

The Role of Safety Protocols in High-Risk Professions

One of the major takeaways from Last Breath is the critical importance of safety protocols in high-risk professions, particularly in industries like deep-sea diving. The documentary and film both stress how even the most carefully laid safety plans can be compromised by unforeseen circumstances, but they also highlight the critical role that these protocols play in preventing accidents from becoming tragedies. In Chris Lemons' case, the tragic incident occurred because of a failure in the underwater infrastructure, but the safety systems and emergency protocols were designed to ensure that he had a chance of surviving in the event of such a disaster.

The use of redundant systems, emergency backup equipment, and constant monitoring of divers' vital signs is a key component of deep-sea diving safety. However, Last Breath also illustrates that even when safety measures are in place, human error or unpredictable circumstances can still present significant risks. The film underscores the need for constant vigilance and adherence to safety procedures to prevent potentially life-threatening situations. In Chris's case, while the incident was unforeseeable, his survival depended on having reliable, well-practiced emergency procedures in place.

In addition to highlighting the physical safety protocols, the film and documentary also explore the psychological aspects of safety in high-risk professions. There is an emotional and mental safety that must be in place among the team members, ensuring they trust one another, communicate effectively, and remain calm in stressful situations. This mental fortitude is as crucial as the physical protocols, especially in high-stakes situations where the mental state of the workers could be the deciding factor in whether or not a tragedy is avoided.

The Power of Teamwork in Survival Situations

Another powerful takeaway from both the documentary and the feature film is the emphasis on teamwork. While Chris Lemons' story is fundamentally about one man's survival, the broader narrative reveals that survival in such extreme conditions is never an individual effort. The rescue team's swift and effective response, the tireless efforts to restore power to the site, and the communication between the surface crew and the divers all played a crucial role in Chris' survival.

In the feature film, the rescue operation is dramatized to emphasize the unity and determination of the team as they race against time to bring Chris back to safety. Each team member plays a specific role in ensuring that Chris' oxygen supply is maintained, his position is located, and the necessary equipment is brought down to the site. The film makes it clear that without this effective teamwork and constant communication, the rescue would have been impossible.

The documentary, while more focused on the personal experience of Chris Lemons, also highlights the crucial importance of teamwork. Interviews with the rescue team show how, even in the face of overwhelming uncertainty and fear, they remained focused on their shared goal: bringing Chris home alive. This sense of camaraderie, despite the risk and danger to their own lives, underscores the importance of collaboration in high-risk professions and serves as a reminder of the human connections that are often the lifeline in such extreme situations.

Broader Reflections on Life and Survival

Beyond the technical and professional lessons, Last Breath offers profound reflections on life and survival. Chris Lemons' harrowing ordeal serves as a metaphor for the ways in which individuals face seemingly insurmountable challenges in life. The isolation he experienced underwater mirrors the isolation many individuals feel when facing personal crises, whether emotional, psychological, or physical. The film and documentary both ask the question: How do we survive in the face of impossible odds? How do we find the strength to continue when there seems to be no hope?

Through Chris' survival, we learn that resilience is not just about physical endurance, but also about mental fortitude and the will to survive. It is about finding meaning in the darkest moments and drawing on every ounce of strength, both physical and psychological, to make it through. Chris Lemons' story is ultimately about the will to live, the human drive to overcome adversity, and the belief that survival, no matter how unlikely, is always possible if one refuses to give up.

In a broader context, Last Breath serves as a reminder of the fragility of life and the unpredictable nature of existence. Whether in the dangerous world of deep-sea diving or in everyday life, it is easy to forget how quickly circumstances can change. The documentary and film urge viewers to reflect on what it means to be alive, to fight for survival, and to rely on the support of others in times of crisis. They encourage an appreciation for the small moments and the relationships that matter most, teaching viewers that survival is not just about enduring; it is about making it through together.

Last Breath is much more than a survival story about deep-sea diving; it is a meditation on the human spirit, resilience, and the power of teamwork in the face of adversity. The documentary and the feature film both offer invaluable lessons about the importance of safety protocols, the dangers of high-risk professions, and the power of trust and collaboration. They also serve as poignant reminders of the psychological toll of isolation, the will to survive against all odds, and the transformative power of human resilience. Ultimately, the lessons of Last Breath apply not just to the world of deep-sea diving but to the many challenges and obstacles that people face in all walks of life.

Chapter Eleven

Cultural and Societal Impact of Last Breath (2019 Documentary & 2025 Feature Film)

Last Breath; both in its documentary form (2019) and its feature film adaptation (2025), has not only captivated audiences with the gripping survival story of Chris Lemons but has also sparked a wider cultural and societal conversation about the high-risk profession of saturation diving and the broader themes of human resilience and survival. This cinematic portrayal has impacted public awareness, shaped perceptions of deep-sea diving, and helped cement Chris Lemons as a symbol of heroism and perseverance. The story of his survival has inspired many, creating ripples beyond the entertainment world into discussions about safety, teamwork, and the psychological and emotional toll of extreme professions.

Public Response to the Documentary and the Feature Film

The Documentary's Reception (2019)

Upon its release, the 2019 documentary Last Breath quickly garnered widespread attention due to the authenticity and emotional depth with which it chronicled Chris Lemons' life-or-death struggle in the North Sea. As a documentary that used real footage and interviews with those directly involved in the incident, it resonated strongly with audiences. Viewers were moved by Chris's emotional journey, as well as the poignant and stark portrayal of the dangers inherent in deep-sea diving. The documentary's raw approach, which included interviews with Chris himself, his colleagues, and experts in the field, created an atmosphere of realism that drew viewers in and made the story relatable despite its extreme nature.

Critically, the documentary was praised for its ability to balance the technical details of saturation diving with the deeply human elements of Chris's struggle. Audiences were impressed by how the filmmakers highlighted not just the physical peril that Chris faced, but also the psychological and emotional toll of his isolation, fear, and hope. The film gave an inside look at the technical side of deep-sea diving and how even the most sophisticated equipment can fail, leaving divers vulnerable to the vast and merciless depths. Furthermore, the documentary provided a stark contrast between the world above the surface, where rescue efforts were underway, and the harrowing conditions below.

Many viewers came away from the documentary with an increased appreciation for the risks associated with deep-sea diving and the unsung heroes who undertake these dangers to help maintain global industry, from underwater construction to oil drilling. In the wake of the film's release, there was a notable increase in discussions about the importance of safety protocols in high-risk professions, and how tragedies like the one Chris Lemons survived could be prevented with further advancements in technology and improved practices.

The Feature Film's Impact (2025)
The 2025 feature film adaptation of Last Breath brought a fictionalized, dramatized version of Chris Lemons' ordeal to a wider audience. The film expanded the narrative, adding more emotional depth and heightened dramatic tension, and included a more comprehensive look at the characters involved in the rescue operation. With a star-studded cast including Woody Harrelson, Simu Liu, and Finn Cole, the movie generated considerable attention from both mainstream audiences and film critics. While the film took creative liberties with certain aspects of the story, its overall goal of conveying the sheer human will to survive remained intact.

Public reaction to the film was largely positive, with many praising the performances, particularly Harrelson's portrayal of the rescue team's leader. However, some viewers and critics noted that the film's dramatization removed some of the documentary's raw authenticity, favoring suspense and cinematic tension over the more grounded, real-life approach of the documentary. Despite this, the film succeeded in drawing attention to the broader issues of workplace safety and the psychological effects of extreme professions. The cinematic format made the story more accessible to a broader demographic, appealing to those who might not typically seek out documentary films.

The emotional impact of the film left audiences reflecting on the nature of human perseverance, sacrifice, and the deep bond of teamwork. This deeper exploration of Chris's relationships with his colleagues and his will to survive became a focal point for discussions, prompting more empathy for people working in high-risk fields. The film's portrayal of isolation, fear, and survival also served as a catalyst for personal reflection, sparking conversations about resilience in the face of adversity.

Influence on Awareness About Saturation Diving

The release of both the documentary and feature film had a significant impact on raising public awareness about the risks and complexities of saturation diving; a profession that most people knew little about before the film's release. Deep-sea diving, especially in the context of offshore oil rigs or underwater infrastructure maintenance, is a niche but highly important industry. The harrowing story of Chris Lemons brought attention to this high-risk profession and allowed the public to understand more clearly the immense dangers faced by those working in these roles.

Saturation diving, as depicted in Last Breath, involves divers living in pressurized environments for weeks, descending to depths of up to 1,000 feet to perform critical operations.

The film emphasized the life-threatening risks associated with the profession, highlighting both the technological marvels that make it possible and the very real dangers involved. Before Last Breath, many were unaware of just how isolated and vulnerable deep-sea divers are, relying on precise coordination between the divers and the support teams on the surface to ensure their survival.

By focusing on Chris Lemons' accident, the film and documentary underscored the complexity of the work involved and highlighted the crucial role of safety protocols, technology, and teamwork in mitigating risks. The intense spotlight on deep-sea diving in both versions of Last Breath helped raise awareness of the industry's challenges, and in some cases, encouraged calls for more stringent regulations, improved safety measures, and increased support for those working in hazardous professions. Chris Lemons' survival serves as both a testament to the effectiveness of such measures and a reminder of the dangers that can still arise despite the most advanced technology.

In the aftermath of the film's release, there were increased discussions in the media and amongst safety advocates about how more could be done to ensure the protection of workers in high-risk industries, particularly in offshore oil drilling and underwater construction. These discussions also extended to the emotional and mental toll on workers, who may not only face physical dangers but also prolonged isolation and extreme stress.

Legacy of Chris Lemons and His Story
Chris Lemons' story, as told through Last Breath, is one of survival against overwhelming odds. His legacy, however, extends far beyond the immediate narrative of his near-death experience. As a real-life hero, Chris Lemons has become an icon of resilience, and his experience serves as an inspiration for people from all walks of life who face their own personal struggles and obstacles.

Chris's legacy also lives on in the positive impact his story has had on the diving industry. His ordeal highlighted the crucial need for continuous improvements in safety protocols and emergency response systems for saturation divers. The focus on Chris's survival has prompted discussions about the emotional and psychological challenges faced by those in high-risk professions, and how mental health should be prioritized alongside physical safety. Chris's resilience under extreme pressure has brought a human face to the statistics and risks involved in these professions, creating an emotional connection that prompts broader societal reflections on workplace safety, human endurance, and the importance of effective support systems.

Moreover, Chris Lemons has used his platform to advocate for better treatment of workers in extreme conditions. His story has helped inspire improvements in safety measures, and his personal advocacy work has raised awareness about the hidden dangers faced by workers in hazardous fields. He has become a symbol not just of survival, but also of the importance of supporting those who put their lives on the line for their work.

In addition to his contributions to the conversation on workplace safety, Chris's story has touched people on a deeply personal level. It serves as a testament to the strength of the human spirit, the power of hope in the darkest moments, and the importance of never giving up. His legacy is a reminder that no matter how bleak the circumstances may seem, there is always a possibility for survival and redemption.

Both the 2019 documentary and the 2025 feature film adaptation of Last Breath have left a lasting cultural and societal impact by raising awareness about the dangers of saturation diving, influencing conversations about safety in high-risk professions, and cementing Chris Lemons' legacy as a symbol of human resilience. Through their portrayal of one man's survival in the face of death, these films have fostered important discussions about teamwork, mental and emotional resilience, and the human capacity to endure unimaginable adversity. Chris Lemons' story continues to inspire and motivate, making a significant mark on both the diving industry and society at large.

Chapter Twelve

Critical Reception and Reviews of Last Breath (2019 Documentary & 2025 Feature Film)

The release of Last Breath in both documentary (2019) and feature film (2025) formats has provoked a significant amount of critical and public attention. Both versions of the film explore the harrowing true story of Chris Lemons, a saturation diver who survived a life-threatening accident in the North Sea. The documentary and feature film, though differing in their formats and dramatic styles, have received varied responses from critics and audiences alike. From the visceral emotional impact of the documentary to the cinematic tension and expanded narrative of the feature film, the reception has been generally favorable but nuanced.

Audience and Critic Responses to the 2019 Documentary

Upon the release of the 2019 documentary Last Breath, the film quickly gained traction with both general audiences and documentary film enthusiasts. The documentary was lauded for its authenticity, emotional resonance, and raw portrayal of Chris Lemons' survival. Viewers were particularly moved by the real footage and interviews with those involved in the rescue efforts, including Lemons himself. The film's ability to balance the technical aspects of deep-sea diving with the personal, emotional journey of Chris Lemons was widely praised. Critics and audiences alike appreciated the documentary's lack of sensationalism and its focus on telling the story in a grounded, realistic way.

One of the standout features of the documentary was its ability to create tension and suspense despite the relatively static nature of the subject matter. The filmmakers expertly used limited footage from the incident itself, along with interviews with those who were there, to construct a gripping narrative. Chris Lemons' personal testimony, where he recounts his experience of near-death and isolation, became a central emotional pillar of the film, giving audiences a sense of connection to his story. The documentary's ability to explore both the technical details of saturation diving and the emotional toll it took on Lemons was widely recognized as one of its strongest points.

However, some critics noted that the documentary's pacing could be slow at times, particularly during the sections where the technical aspects of the diving process were discussed in greater detail. While this aspect provided valuable context for understanding the challenges of the profession, some viewers felt that it detracted from the emotional immediacy of the story. Still, the overall consensus was that Last Breath was a deeply impactful and well-executed documentary that successfully shed light on the often-overlooked dangers of deep-sea diving. It was not just a story of survival but one of resilience, teamwork, and the importance of human connection in extreme circumstances.

The documentary's critical acclaim helped establish Last Breath as a standout in the genre of survival documentaries. It received positive reviews from outlets such as The Guardian, The Hollywood Reporter, and Variety, which praised its emotional depth, focus on human perseverance, and unflinching portrayal of the risks associated with high-risk professions. The film also sparked conversations in the diving community, leading to greater discussions about safety measures, regulations, and the mental health challenges faced by those in extreme occupations.

Early Reviews and Expectations for the 2025 Feature Film

Last Breath: A Tale of Survival in the Depths

When it was announced that a feature film adaptation of Last Breath was in the works, anticipation began to build. With director Alex Parkinson at the helm, known for his work on both documentaries and high-stakes narratives, the feature film adaptation was expected to bring a more dramatic and cinematic approach to Chris Lemons' story. The 2025 feature film, starring a high-profile cast including Woody Harrelson, Simu Liu, and Finn Cole, had already attracted significant attention before its release due to the star power involved and the high expectations set by the success of the documentary.

Early reviews for the feature film were largely positive, though they revealed a mixed response to the film's dramatization of real events. While many praised the visual and sound effects used to recreate the underwater environment and the high level of tension maintained throughout the film, others felt that the dramatization detracted from the authenticity and emotional weight that the documentary had achieved. The feature film's decision to add fictionalized characters and expand on the emotional lives of the supporting characters was seen as both a strength and a weakness. While this allowed for a deeper exploration of the dynamics between the characters and added more human drama, some critics felt that it moved away from the documentary's more grounded, minimalist approach.

One of the key points of comparison between the documentary and feature film was the decision to portray Chris Lemons not just as a survivor, but as a heroic figure who must overcome immense psychological and emotional obstacles in addition to the physical dangers he faces. While the documentary focused on his recounting of events and the real footage of the rescue, the feature film took creative liberties to enhance the personal struggles Lemons faced. Critics were divided on this aspect, with some praising the film for creating a more dynamic, emotionally charged version of the story, while others felt that it undermined the raw emotional power of the real-life account.

Despite these differences, the general expectation for the feature film was that it would draw more mainstream audiences, as the film medium is often more accessible and appealing to a wider demographic. The use of star actors and a larger budget for visual effects also set the stage for a more visually stunning retelling of the story, though some fans of the documentary expressed concern that the film might not live up to the more restrained, authentic approach of the original documentary.

Awards and Accolades

Both the documentary and feature film versions of Last Breath have garnered significant attention from film festivals, critics, and award bodies.

The 2019 Documentary's Recognition

The 2019 documentary received critical acclaim and earned several prestigious nominations and awards. It was praised for its integrity, its deep exploration of human endurance, and its ability to translate a technical subject into a gripping, emotional story. It made its rounds through numerous film festivals, including the Tribeca Film Festival and Hot Docs Canadian International Documentary Festival, where it was well-received by audiences and critics alike. At Tribeca, the documentary received the award for Best Documentary Feature, and its emotional resonance earned it special recognition in various outlets.

The film's careful balance of technical insight and personal storytelling set it apart from many other survival documentaries. The decision to focus on the human side of the story, without overly relying on dramatic re-enactments or sensationalism, helped it stand out in an often crowded genre. Many film critics noted its ability to humanize the otherwise cold, mechanical world of deep-sea diving, and it won several awards for Best Editing and Best Cinematography in Documentary.

The 2025 Feature Film's Early Buzz

As for the 2025 feature film, early buzz surrounding its release included expectations that it would become a major contender in the upcoming award season. Given the involvement of high-profile actors and the visual spectacle of the underwater scenes, there was significant anticipation for it to be recognized in the categories of Best Cinematography and Best Visual Effects. Critics anticipated that the movie would perform well in awards circuits, particularly in the realms of drama and survival narratives.

In the lead-up to its premiere, early reviews suggested the film was likely to generate nominations for its performances, with particular attention being paid to Woody Harrelson's portrayal of the rescue team leader and Finn Cole's dramatic turn as a fellow diver. Early screenings indicated that the movie's emotional power would likely make it a contender for several accolades in categories such as Best Actor and Best Director.

The critical reception and reviews for both Last Breath (2019 documentary) and Last Breath (2025 feature film) highlight the strengths and weaknesses inherent in both versions of the story. The documentary's emotional depth and grounded, factual approach earned it widespread acclaim and a number of prestigious awards, while the feature film, with its larger-than-life cinematic style, has garnered early praise for its star performances and intense visual presentation. Both versions offer unique insights into the human spirit and survival, with the documentary remaining an authentic, raw representation of Chris Lemons' real-life experience, while the feature film draws on creative dramatization to amplify the story's emotional and cinematic impact. The success of both versions in garnering critical attention and accolades underscores the power of Chris Lemons' story and its enduring appeal across different formats.

Conclusion

Final Thoughts on Last Breath as a Compelling Story of Survival

Last Breath is an extraordinary and gripping account of survival that transcends the technical aspects of deep-sea diving to focus on the human experience in life-or-death situations. Both the 2019 documentary and the 2025 feature film adaptation offer powerful, albeit different, representations of Chris Lemons' near-fatal accident while working as a saturation diver in the North Sea. The heart of the story is not just the perilous circumstances Lemons faced, but his resilience, determination, and the invaluable support from his colleagues that made his survival possible. The story's emotional depth, coupled with its technical precision, makes Last

Breath a compelling narrative of survival, courage, and hope.

From the documentary's raw, real-time portrayal of the harrowing ordeal to the cinematic expansion in the feature film, Last Breath offers a unique exploration of what it means to confront death and fight for life. The real-life nature of the story, combined with Chris Lemons' personal testimony, makes the documentary an unflinching exploration of human endurance in extreme conditions. The feature film, while dramatizing certain elements, continues to highlight the universal themes of teamwork, trust, and the bond between colleagues in high-risk professions. These themes resonate far beyond the world of deep-sea diving, offering viewers a powerful lesson in the strength of the human spirit.

The documentary's enduring legacy lies in its authenticity and emotional power. By focusing on the real people involved, the documentary captured a level of rawness and sincerity that resonated deeply with audiences. It illuminated the often unseen dangers of deep-sea diving and brought awareness to the mental and physical toll that such high-risk professions can take on individuals. The film's success also sparked broader discussions about safety protocols, mental health, and the importance of teamwork in high-stakes environments.

The feature film, while more dramatized, expands the narrative in ways that make the story accessible to a wider audience. It introduces new characters and emotional layers, building on the themes of resilience and survival. Though the dramatization of certain events may take liberties, the core message of the human will to survive remains intact. The feature film's visual style, with stunning underwater cinematography and a star-studded cast, adds a cinematic grandeur to the story that complements the more intimate approach of the documentary.

Both versions of Last Breath offer valuable insights into the extremes of human survival. The documentary serves as a raw, factual account, while the feature film elevates the story with cinematic flair, both making strong cases for the importance of teamwork and resilience in the face of insurmountable odds.

Recommendation for Viewers
For those interested in real-life survival stories, Last Breath is an essential watch. The 2019 documentary is highly recommended for viewers seeking an authentic, emotionally powerful account of one man's fight for survival against all odds. It provides an insightful, honest look at the risks faced by deep-sea divers and highlights the importance of safety, mental strength, and collaboration in extreme situations.

The 2025 feature film is recommended for those who enjoy dramatic retellings of true stories with heightened emotional and visual intensity. While it takes creative liberties, it successfully conveys the spirit of the original story, offering an engaging and suspenseful experience.

In any form, Last Breath stands as a testament to human resilience and the incredible capacity for survival in the face of nearly unimaginable challenges. Whether you prefer a factual, documentary-style approach or a more cinematic dramatization, this story is one that will leave a lasting impression on viewers.